J
743.697   Ames, Lee J.
A   Draw 50 horses / Lee J. Ames. -- 1st ed. --
            Garden City, N.Y. : Doubleday, c1984.

            [61] p. : ill. ; bkl 2-4

            SUMMARY: Step-by-step instructions for
            drawing different breeds of horses in a
            variety of poses.
            ISBN 0-385-17641-4(lib. bdg.) : $9.95

                              83445

            1. Horses in art. 2. Animal painting and
            illustration. 3. Drawing--Technique.   I.
            Title.
                                          NOV 8 7

                                      81-43646 /AC

Other Doubleday books by Lee J. Ames:

DRAW, DRAW, DRAW
DRAW 50 ANIMALS
DRAW 50 BOATS, SHIPS, TRUCKS AND TRAINS
DRAW 50 DINOSAURS AND OTHER PREHISTORIC ANIMALS
DRAW 50 AIRPLANES, AIRCRAFT AND SPACECRAFT
DRAW 50 FAMOUS FACES
DRAW 50 FAMOUS CARTOONS
DRAW 50 VEHICLES
DRAW 50 BUILDINGS AND OTHER STRUCTURES
DRAW 50 DOGS
DRAW 50 FAMOUS STARS
DRAW 50 MONSTERS, CREEPS, SUPERHEROES, DEMONS,
          DRAGONS, NERDS, DIRTS, GHOULS, GIANTS,
          VAMPIRES, ZOMBIES, AND OTHER CURIOSA...
DRAW 50 ATHLETES
DRAW 50 CARS, TRUCKS, BIKES AND MOTORCYCLES
MAKE 25 CRAYON DRAWINGS OF THE CIRCUS
MAKE 25 FELT-TIP DRAWINGS OUT WEST
THE DOT, LINE AND SHAPE CONNECTION

Draw **50** Horses

Draw 50 Horses

Lee J. Ames

Doubleday & Company, Inc.

Garden City, New York

ISBN: 0-385-17640-6 Trade
        0-385-17641-4 Prebound
        0-385-17642-2 Paperback

Text and Illustrations copyright © 1984 by Lee J. Ames and Murray D. Zak

Library of Congress Cataloging in Publication Data
Ames, Lee J.
    Draw 50 horses.
    Summary: Step-by-step instructions for drawing different breeds of horses
in a variety of poses.
    1. Horses in art — Juvenile literature. 2. Drawing — Technique —
Juvenile literature. [1. Horses in art. 2. Animal painting and illustration.
3. Drawing — Technique] I. Title. II. Title: Draw fifty horses.
NC783.8.H65A43   1984   743'.69725   81-43646
    9 8 7 6 5 4

To Alison, regal and elegant . . .

. . . and thank you, Tamara Scott, for your help.

To the Reader

Broncos, Arabians, thoroughbreds, dancers and prancers —here they all are. By following simple, step-by-step instructions, you can draw them.

Start by gathering your equipment. You will need paper, medium and/or soft pencils, and a kneaded eraser (available at art supply stores). You might also wish to use India ink, a fine brush or pen, or perhaps a fine pointed felt-tip or ball-point pen.

Next, choose one of the horses...you needn't start with the first illustration. As you begin, remember that the first few steps—the foundation of the drawing—are the most important. If they are not right, the end result will be distorted. So, follow these steps *very carefully* and keep your lines *very* light. In order that they can be clearly seen, these steps are shown darker in this book than you should draw them. You can lighten your lines by gently pressing them with the kneaded eraser.

Make sure step one is accurate before you go on to step two. To check your own accuracy, hold the work up to a mirror after a few steps. By reversing the image, the mirror gives you a new view of the drawing. If you haven't done it quite right, you may notice that your drawing is out of proportion or off to one side.

You can reinforce the drawing by going over the completed final step with India ink and a fine brush or pen; or with the felt-tip or ball-point. When the ink has dried thoroughly, gently remove the pencil lines with the kneaded eraser.

Don't get discouraged if, at first, you find it difficult to duplicate the shapes pictured. Just keep at it, and in no time you'll be able to make the pencil go just where you wish. Drawing, like any other skill, requires patience, practice, and perseverance.

Remember, this book presents only one method of drawing. In a most enjoyable way, it will help you develop a certain skill and control. But there are many other ways of drawing to which you can apply this skill, and the more of them you explore, the more interesting your drawings will be.

Lee J. Ames

To the Parent or Teacher

Drawing, like any other skill, requires practice and discipline. But this does not mean that rewards cannot be found along every step of the way.

While contemporary methods of art instruction rightly emphasize freedom of expression and experimentation, they often lose sight of a very basic, traditional and valuable approach: the "follow me, step by step" way that I learned as a youth.

Just as a beginning musician is given simple, beautiful melodies to play, so too the young artist needs to gain a sense of satisfaction and pride in his/her work as soon as possible. The "do as I do" steps that I have laid out here provide the opportunity to mimic finished images, pictures the young artist is eager to draw.

Mimicry is prerequisite for developing creativity. We learn the use of our tools through mimicry, and once we have those tools we are free to express ourselves in whatever fashion we choose. The use of this book will help lay a solid foundation for the child, one that can be continued with other books in the Draw 50 series, or even used to complement different approaches to drawing.

Above all, the joy of making a credible, attractive image will encourage the child to continue and grow as an artist, giving him even more of a sense of pride and accomplishment when his friends say, "Peter can draw a horse better than anyone else!"

Lee J. Ames

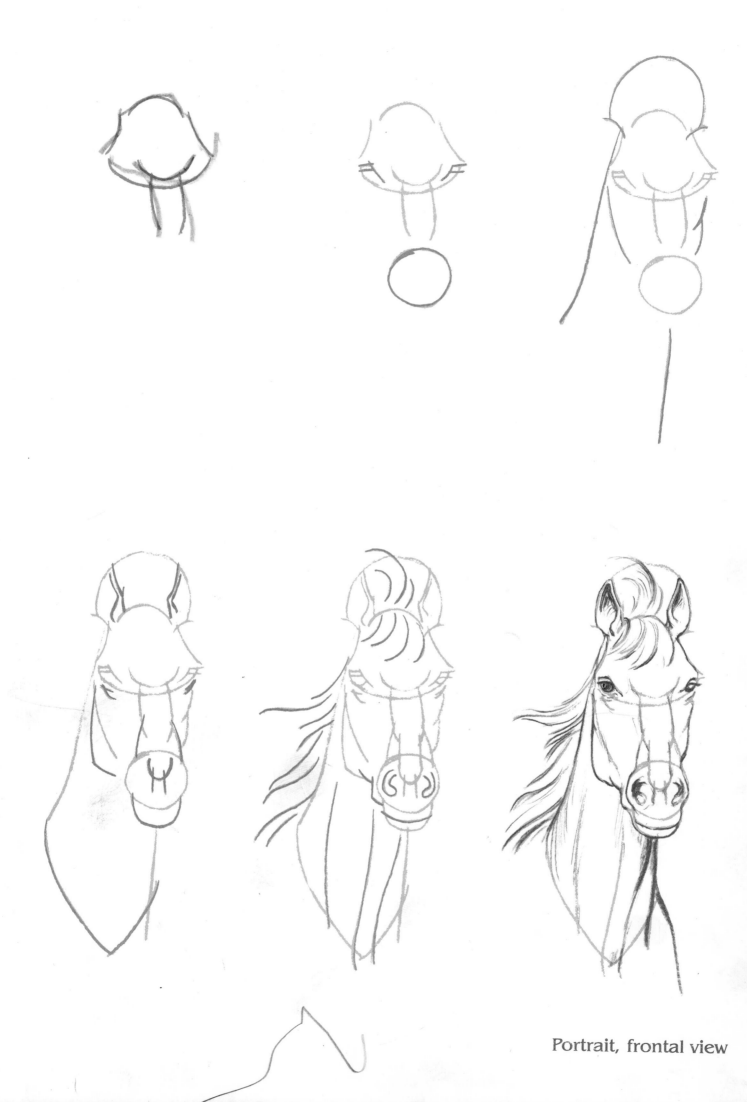

Portrait, frontal view

Portrait, side view

Portrait, side view

Portrait, rearing

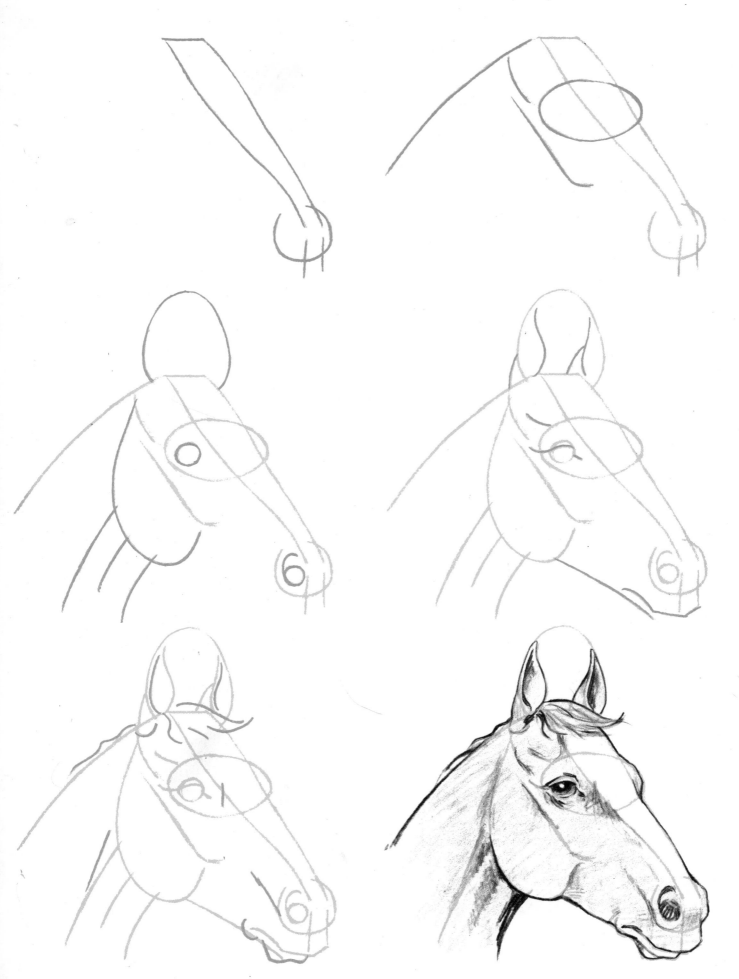

Portrait, blaze

Portrait, nag

Arabian

Percheron

Clydesdale

Morgan

Shire

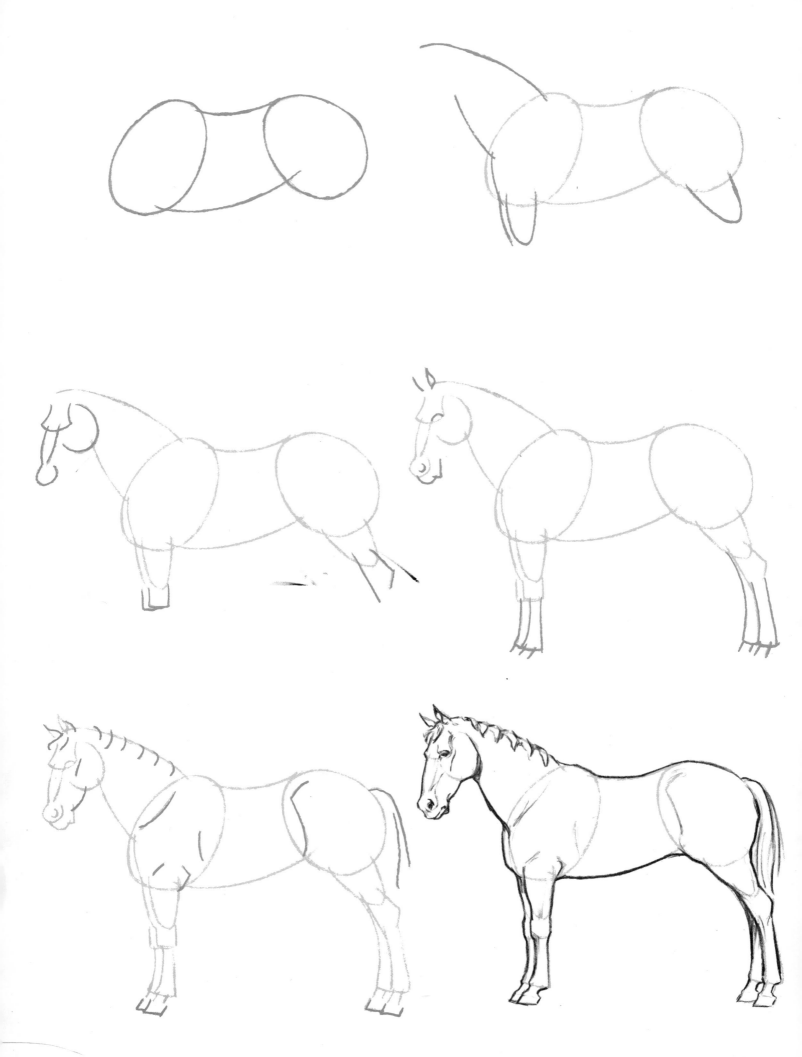

Tennessee Walking Horse

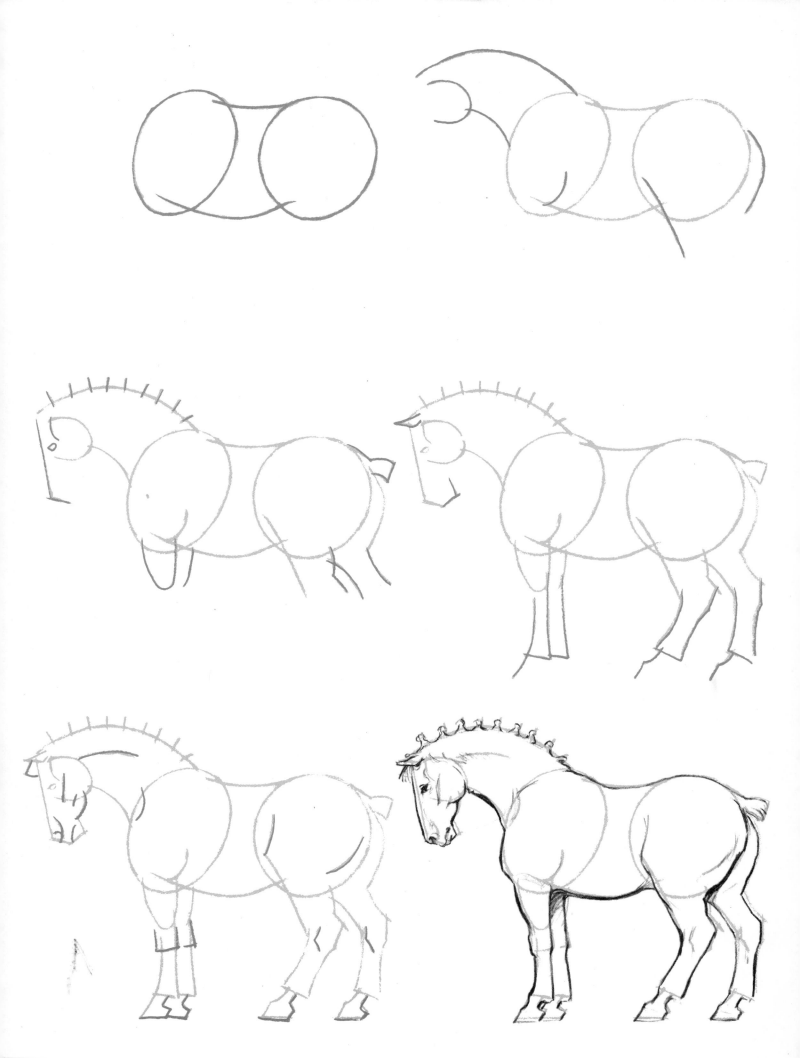

Belgian

American Saddle Horse

Shetland Pony

Thoroughbred

Przhevalski (wild Asian horse)

Appaloosa

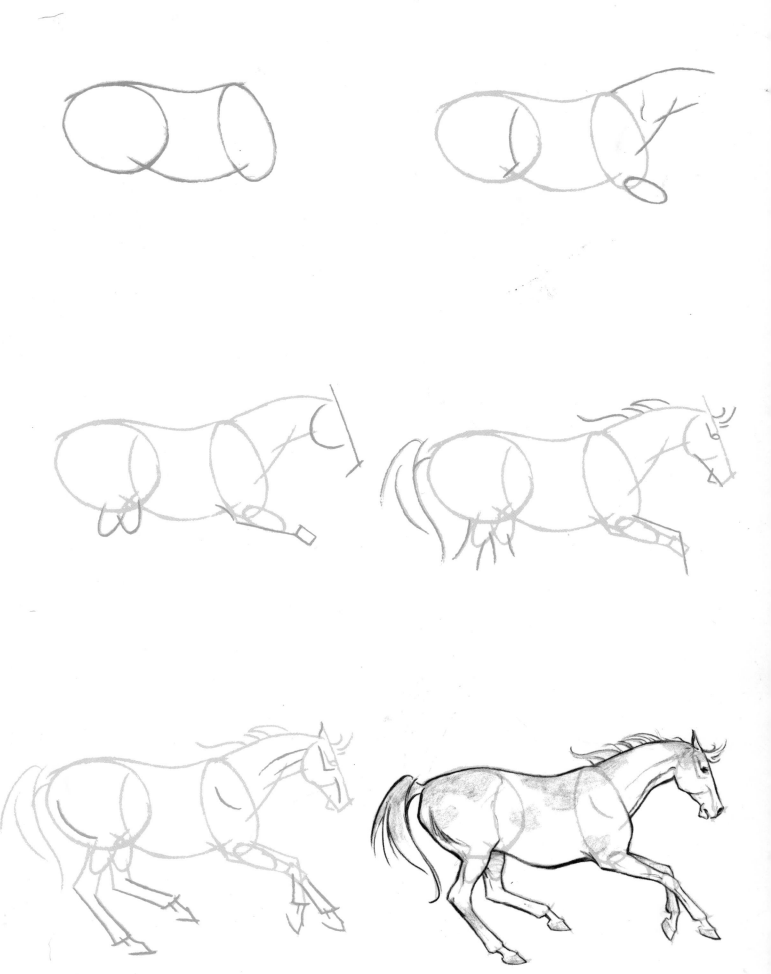

Pinto

Performing Lippizaner, Levade

Performing Lippizaner, Capriole

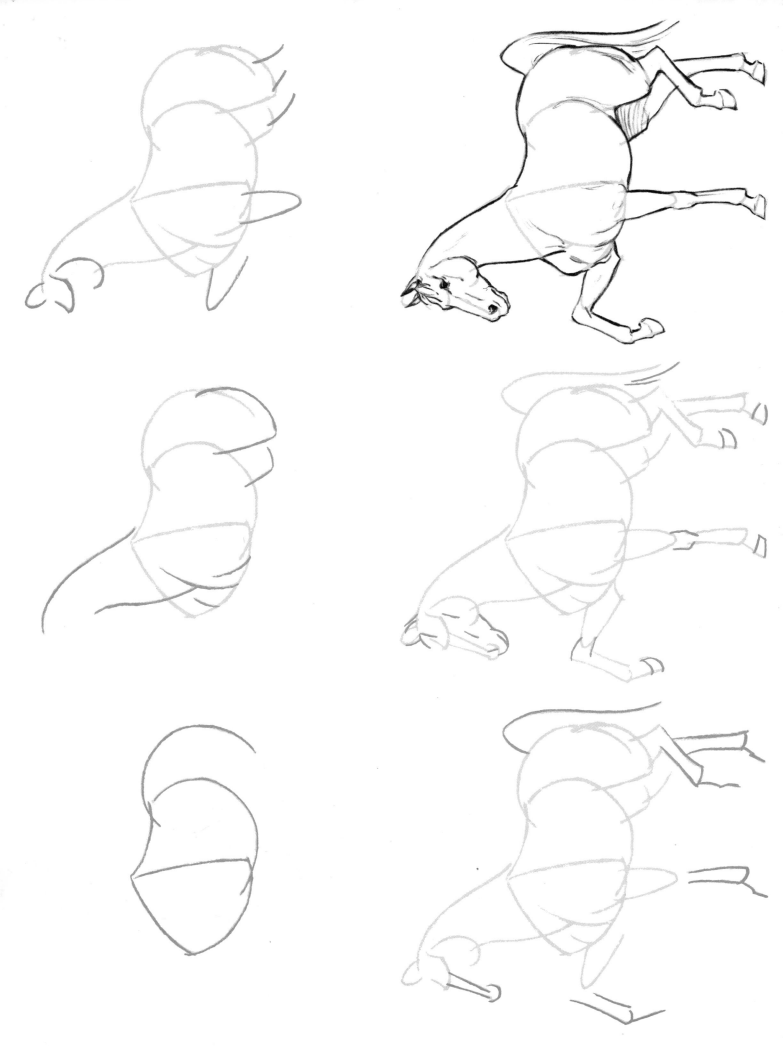

Performing Lippizaner, Piaffe

Tennessee Walking Horse, High-Stepping

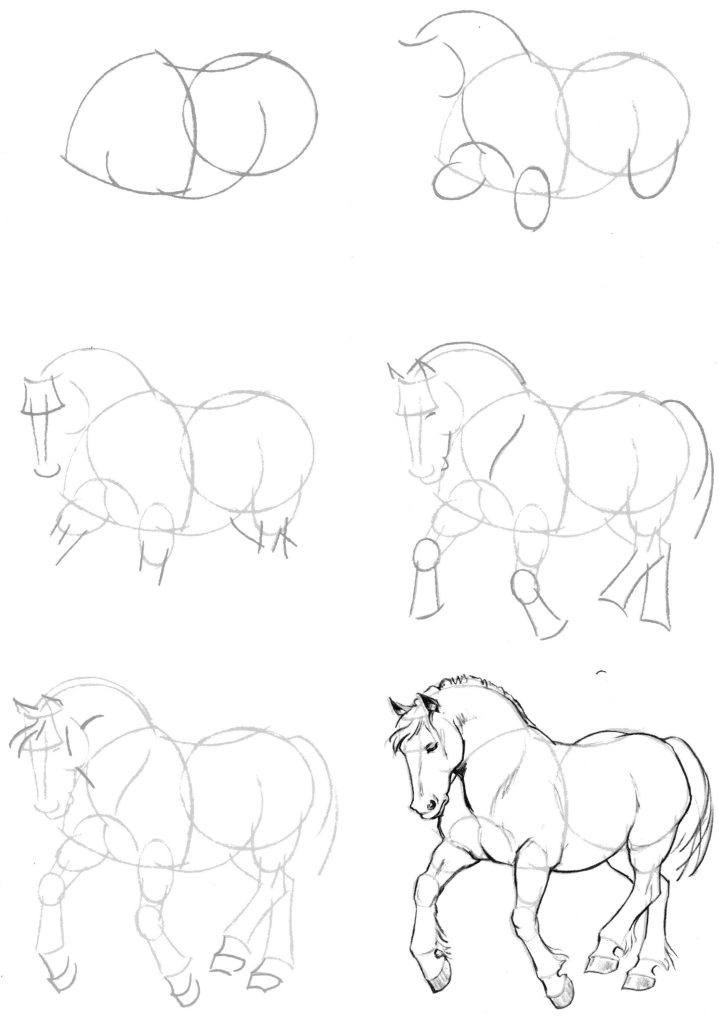

Workhorse

Workhorse at the canter

Workhorse at the walk

Jumping #1

Jumping #2

Jumping #3

Jumping #4

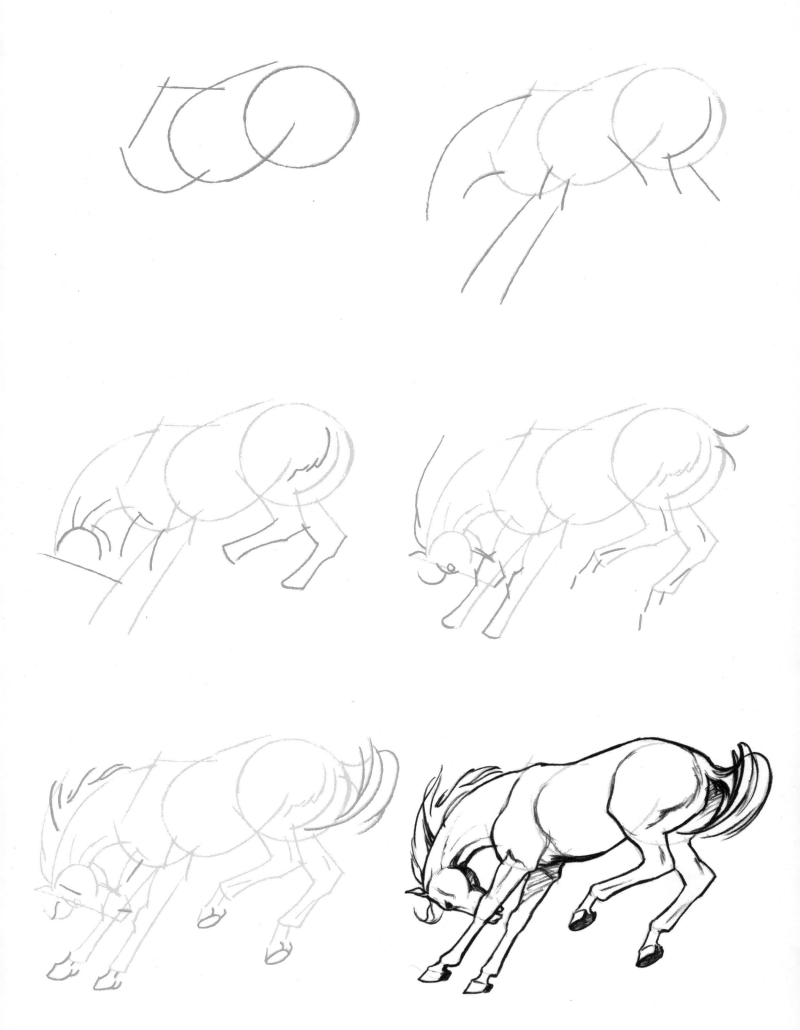

Bucking #1

Bucking #2

Bucking #3

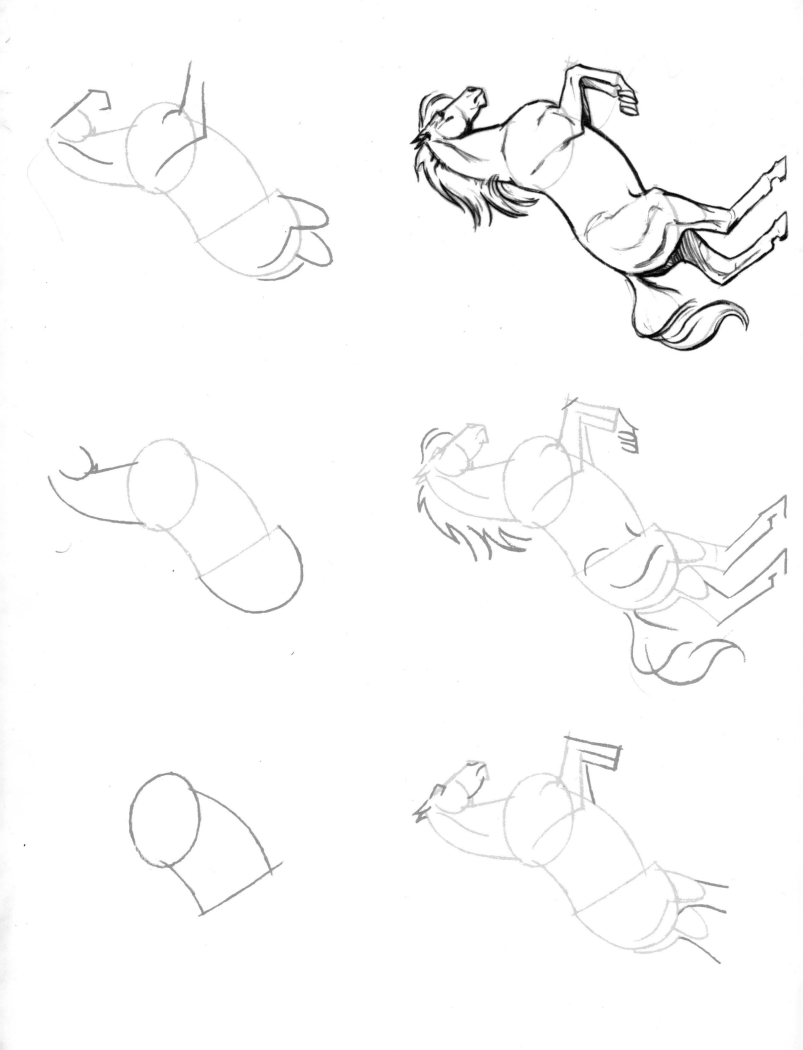

Rearing, side view

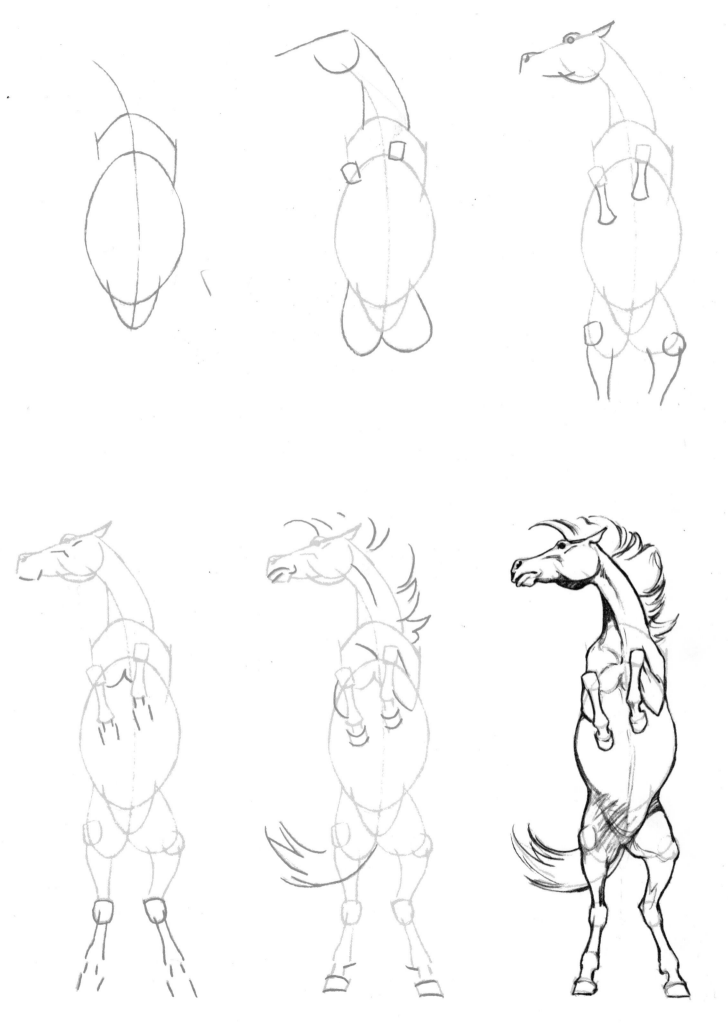

Rearing, front view

Shying

Kicking

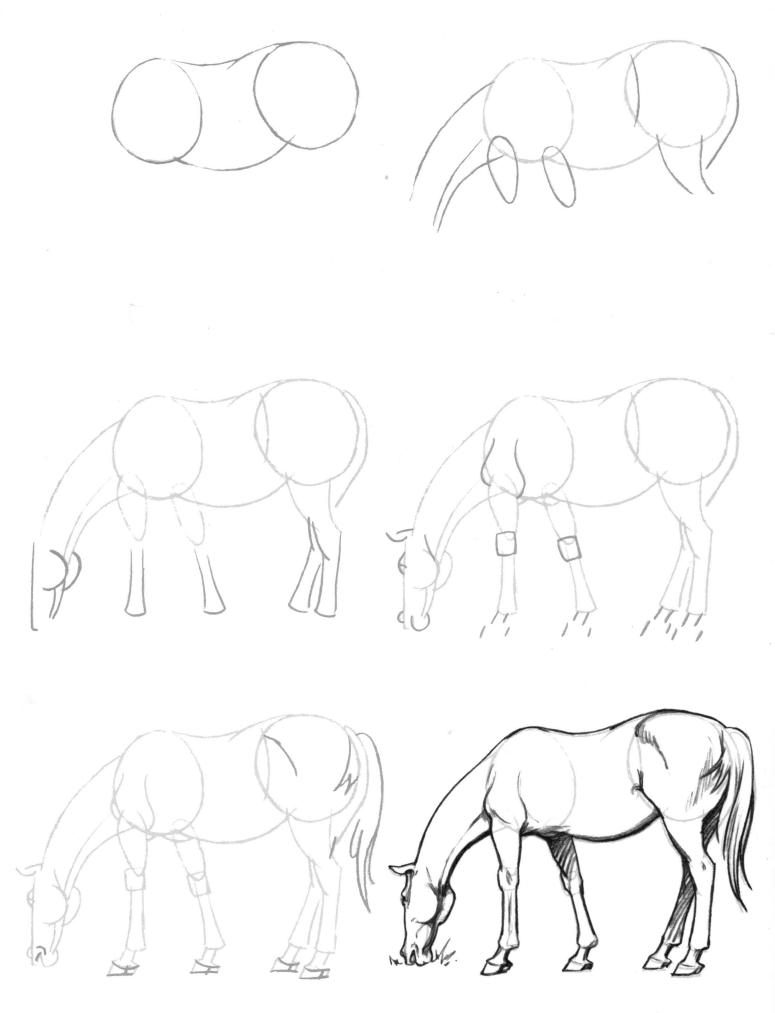

Grazing

Standing, rear view

Standing, side view

Walking, three-quarter view

Walking, side view

Trotting, side view

Trotting, rear view

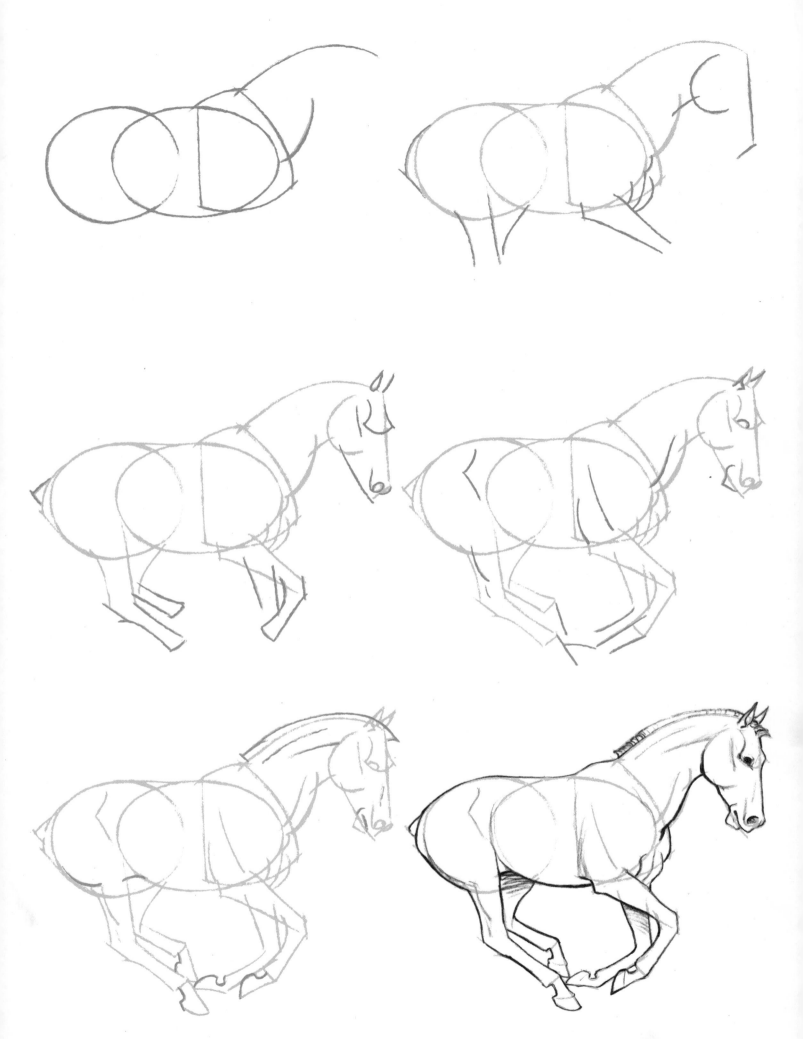

Cantering #1

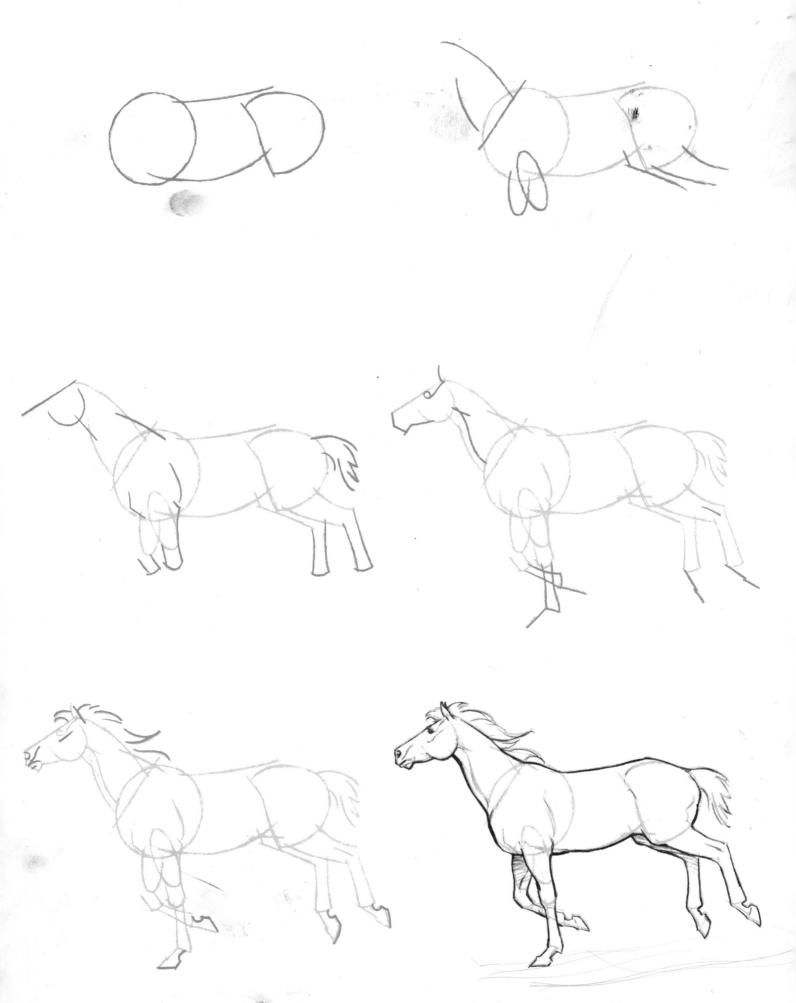

Cantering #2

Galloping, rear view

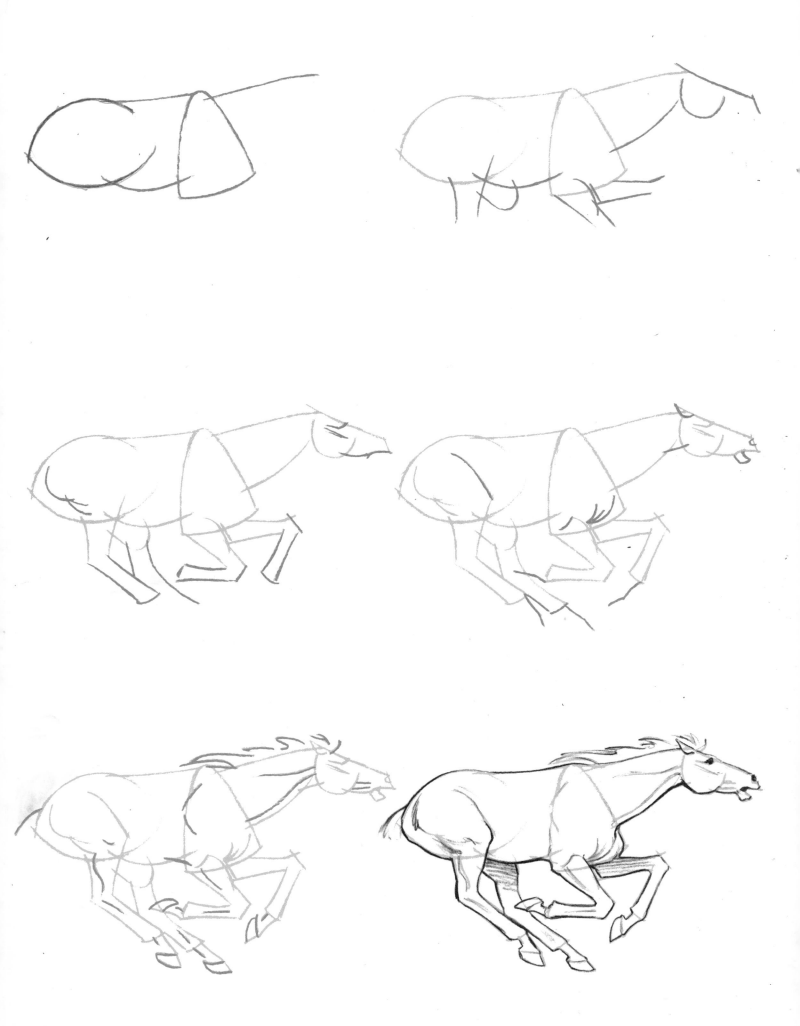

Galloping, side view

Colt

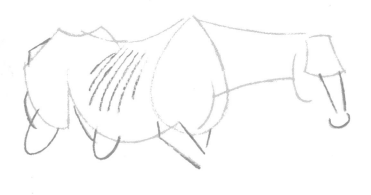

Old Age

Lee J. Ames has been earning his living as an artist for almost forty years. He began his career working on Walt Disney's *Fantasia* and *Pinocchio.* He has taught at the School of Visual Arts in Manhattan and, more recently, at Dowling College on Long Island. He was, for a time, director of his own advertising agency and illustrator for several magazines. Mr. Ames has illustrated over one hundred books, from preschool picture books to postgraduate texts. When not working, he battles on the tennis court. A native New Yorker, Lee J. Ames lives in Dix Hills, Long Island, with his wife, Jocelyn, their three dogs, and a calico cat.